The Folly of God

*S*ieger Köder was born on 3rd January 1925 in Wasseralfingen, Germany, where he also completed his high school studies.

During the Second World War, Sieger Köder was sent to France as a front line soldier; there he was made a prisoner of war in 1944-45. Once freed, Köder studied engraving and silversmithing. He attended the Academy School of Art in Stuttgart until 1951 and then studied English philology at the University of Tübigen as part of his qualification as a teacher.

After 12 years of teaching art and working as an artist, Köder undertook theological studies for the priesthood, and in 1971 he was ordained a Catholic priest. From 1975 to 1995, Fr Köder was a parish priest in Hohenberg and in Rosenberg. He then retired in Ellwangen, not far from Stuttgart, where he now lives.

The years of Köder's parish ministry are among the most prolific with inspiring works of art. There is complete synergy between Fr Köder being a minister and an artist. He uses his paintings as Jesus used his parables. He reveals the depth of the Christian message through metaphors and by shedding light and colour on human history. Thus we understand why Köder's art is heavily charged with the experience the Nazi period and the time of the Holocaust.

Köder's paintings are also rich with theological insight. He shows a certain reserve

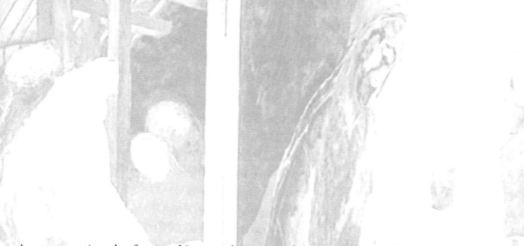

in representing the figure of Jesus, who most of the time is outside the scene – in the position of the viewer – to convey the idea that Jesus is alive today in the person of the viewer.

One of his leitmotif is the Harlequin. A counterpart of the modern robot – a creation of rationality, logic, planning, and precision – the Harlequin symbolises irrationality, poetry, freedom, amusement... The Harlequin stands for art and for the artist. Furthermore, behind its comic façade there is the reality of each one of us. In fact, "We are all fools", states Sieger Köder. Maybe the Harlequin stands also for the folly of God?

Köder dips his brush into the very essence of the Gospel and with colour describes the wholeness of human life. Thus, his art is a vibrant glimpse of the depth, the length and the width of the mystery of Christ in each one of us.

We feel privileged to have been given the opportunity to reproduce an important, though partial, collection of Fr Köder's paintings and to offer them to you in a very accessible format for personal and group meditation. We present them to you in the hope of supporting your exploration and contemplation of the Word of God.

The images in this publication and more of Sieger Köder's paintings that are not included in *The Folly of God* collection are also available as posters and in other formats. For information please visit our online catatlogue at *www.pauline-uk.org*

God's folly
is wiser
than
human wisdom,
and
God's
weakness
is stronger
than
human strength.

first Corinthians chapter one verse twenty-five

*W*e found no better title to embrace this remarkable collection of works by Sieger Köder, based on the events of the passion and resurrection of Jesus. The artist seems both mesmerised and fascinated by this paradox: the mystery of Christ made one with the mystery of humanity.

As we meditate on the life of Christ, we are challenged by the mystery of the cross and the unconditional love of God. It is difficult to come to terms with the paradox of the cross. How can one who ended his life upon a cross be the Son of God? Our mind refuses to deal with that which sounds a contradiction in terms. Christ is the paradox of God and his cross is a mystery to us. In fact, in Jesus' time as well as in our own times, for many the cross may be a stumbling block.

But for those who have faith, as Paul says, 'Christ is the power of God and God's weakness is stronger than human strength'. This is the logic of love. Perhaps we can better grasp this great mystery when we experience love in our lives; then we know how ready we are to give ourselves for the sake of the person we love. God is infinitely greater than our heart and Jesus is the measure of his love for us.

We sincerely hope that both the images and the reflections in this booklet may help us all to grow in the understanding of how much we are loved by God. May we also draw strength and insight from the *folly* of the cross.

This booklet offers reflective thought, prayer and scripture refrences to open up our understanding of the symbolism of each of the 18 images. In our visually saturated culture, the work of Sieger Köder is invaluable as a resource for prayer, liturgy and group sessions.

These 18 images unfold the paschal mystery of the passion, death and resurrection of Jesus. The second to the fifteenth image feature the traditional stations of the *Way of the Cross*.

*I lift up my
eyes to the
mountains;
where is my help
to come from?*

Psalm 121:1

wonder

His glorified body translucent
Greeted by seekers from of old,
The long awaited Messiah
Now revealed in all his splendour.
The old covenant
Is sealed with the new.

Watching from below
From the world of mortals
The three disciples are blessed
With a glimpse of heaven.

On the Mountain top.
The light from the world of the living
Penetrates the shell of the body
And they can see with their inner eyes,
The awe-inspiring vision.

It is so good to be here,
Blissfully content in God's splendour –
The glory of the beloved Son.

Listen to him!

The Son of Man has to suffer
To enter his glory.

Death is only the doorway.
We can now see him
As in a mirror.
Then we shall see him as he really is.
We shall be forever
In the splendour of God's glory.

wonder

The Transfiguration manifests the profound and wonderful reality that we are partakers in the glory of the children of God. The radiance of Tabor projects light over the shadow of our world, charged with the reality of suffering and death. It shows a thrust, which is more powerful than our desperation; a sun which will never set.

Jesus told us that he came so that we may have joy, a superabundant joy. The vision of Tabor is an experience open to each one of us when we are in touch in our inmost self, with God. It is a gratuitous gift, a divine enlightenment, a glimpse of our real destiny.

On the mountain, close to God, though tired of our journeying into life, Jesus invites us to look upon him. To see him as the risen Lord, who holds power over suffering and death. He is the Lord of the living.

themes and scripture
A Path to Light

- Wonder
  Mt 17:1-8; Mk 9:2-8; Lk 9:28-36; 2 Pt 1:16-18

- The hour of shadow and light
  Jn 11:25-26; 12:20-36; Rm 8:18-30; 2 Cor 3:1-4:5; Ph 3:20-21

We pray...

God our Father,

in your son Jesus

you reveal to us

the wonder of your glory.

Strengthen our faith

so that,

even when we are

confronted with pain

and death,

the splendour

of your glory

may shine in us.

They led Jesus off
to the house
of Caiaphas,
the high priest...
Pilate took
some water,
washed his hands
and said,
'I am innocent
of this man's blood'.

Matthew 26: 57. 27: 24

surrender

Three figures.
Three worlds.
On trial!

Possessive hands
Holding the scrolls of the Law.
Detached with unconnecting eyes –
Priestly garments.

A seemingly harsh will of God
That the innocent
Should die for all.
Is this relying on God?
Is it not rather an escape,
Manipulation?
In God's name!

Washing hands,
Corrupting pure water
With blood.

One day, that water
Had been changed into wine
To gladden the hearts.
Now, becomes blood of betrayal.

Truth?
What is the truth
Behind that masked face,
That furtive look?
The truth you refuse to see
The power you don't want to lose.
The truth?

Here is the man!

The obedient servant.
Mute like a lamb.
His ear attentive
His back,
Stripped of the regal garments,
Offered to violent blows.
His face at peace,
In the heart a song:
Here I am,
I come to do your will!

surrender

Where can we find real strength, where is the truth? In those with positions of power, or in the One whose head is bowed, whose arms are lowered in peace, only being raised when nailed to the cross?

How many innocent people pay the price of dishonesty, of abuse of power? Even by those who act in God's name. Indeed by anyone who manipulates the truth of the gospel to justify violence, non-involvement, refusal of truth. How ready we all are to surrender to hypocrisy and to hide behind the mask of our lack of courage. We would rather not get involved, distance ourselves from the wrong we see around us. Keep silence in the face of injustice inflicted on our brothers and sisters: friends, colleagues, neighbours and loved ones... All we want is to keep our name clean, our reputation untarnished.

themes and scripture

The Journey of the Cross | 1st Station | Jesus is condemned

- Surrender
  Mk15:12-15 (Song of the Servant Is 42:1-4; 49:1-4; 50:4-11; 53:10-12)

- Truth makes us free
  Jn 8:31-36; Rm 6:17-19; Gal 5:13

- Authority and responsibility
  Ps 28:1-2; Mt 20:24-29. 23:1-12; Mk 10:41-45; Lk 11:46. 22:24-27; Jn 5:19-40

We pray...

Jesus, you didn't hesitate

to pay the price

of our wrongdoing.

Give us the courage

to face the truth

when we fail.

Give us strength

to be true

to your gospel

and to be true

to our brothers

and sisters.

Carrying his own cross, he went out to the Place of the Skull, as it is called in Hebrew, Golgotha.

John 19: 17

embrace

Naked heavy wood
Embraced tenderly
By bleeding, bare hands.
Crimson garments soaked
With streams of red blood.

The wood is steady, firm.
On it heavily leans
Another piece of wood –
The cross.

In the background, hanging nooses
Reminders of violence and war,
Indisputable witnesses to
Generations of innocent victims.
Yesterday, today!

Two hands embracing
An unjust verdict,
Human sorrow.

A destiny shared,
A cry hidden behind the cross –
The Innocent One.

embrace

I t takes courage to embrace that which we really would rather not. To reach out each day in our world of violence and atrocities. To make a decision to accept Jesus and the paradox of his cross.

Our hands are a precious gift. We can create or destroy, lift up or force down. We can embrace or push away. Jesus used his hands to bless, to gather the lost into his arms, all the time announcing the Good News, bringing peace. Until finally he opened his hands to the cross. Accepting and embracing it, he embraces our sorrows, our cross.

themes and scripture

The Journey of the Cross | **2ⁿᵈ Station** | **Jesus embraces the cross**

- Embrace
  Ps 40:6-10; Jr 20:7; Mt 7:21. 12:50; Mk 14:36; Jn 4:34; Hb 10:5-10

- The measure of love
  Jn 3:16.15:12-14; Rm 5:6-8; Ph 2:5-11

We pray...

Lord Jesus,

the mystery

of your cross

is at the heart

of our lives.

Help us embrace

the world as you did.

Give us the perseverance

we need to make

our world a better place.

Your kingdom come,

your will be done.

19

Crushed,
because of our guilt.
The punishment
reconciling us
fell on him,
and we have been
healed by
his bruises.

cf Isaiah 53:5-7

cornerstone

On your knees
Under the cry of the world
Heavily weighing on you,
The pillar of the universe.

Darkness and horror plunge
Onto the wood of your cross –
The implacable grim-faced judge,
The tormented bodies of the victims
Of violence and vices:
The sin of the world.

On your knees.
The translucent flesh
Stained with blood.
Your right arm firmly strained
Unbent, steady
Like a pillar beam.

The right hand, firmly planted
Over the solid stone –
Supporting, securing…

The head leaning on your heart,
The source of your strength.
Determined as you are
To lose none of the little ones
Entrusted to you.
You the cornerstone,
You the pillar of the universe.
You, carry us all.

cornerstone

We all know the feeling: *I can't go on.* The very life is being squeezed out of us. Lack of love in our lives can weigh us down. When we are rejected we become vulnerable. We neither respect others nor ourselves. We become violent and abusive towards those who are more vulnerable than we are. Our human dignity is lost, and we condemn ourselves to shame and degradation.

Jesus died to save us from ourselves. He took away the sin of the world. He restored in us the likeness of the children of God.

themes and scripture

The Journey of the Cross | 3rd **Station** | The first fall of Jesus

- Cornerstone
  Ps 118:22; Is 53:4-5; 2 Cor 5:21; Hb 2:10; 1 Pt 2:24

- In Jesus is our strength
  Is 53:3-12; Ph 2:5-11; Hb 2:14-15; 5:2-3

We pray...

Jesus, you bore

our sin

so that we might live.

You are the rock

of our strength.

Do not allow us

to neglect those

who are crushed

by their own mistakes,

those who feel rejected,

the sinful.

*His mother
kept all these things
in her heart.*

Luke 2: 51

no words

Two figures
Bound together by the vigorous wood,
Firmly standing between them.
Two lives tied as one
By the same destiny.

Two persons identifiable only,
One, by the scarlet regal garment;
The other, by the green clothing,
The mourning veil.
A mother and child?
So intimate.

What is the emotion depicted on their faces?
What are the words they utter to each other?
Do they lean on each other's shoulders?
Does the mother caress her child's cheek?
Does the child comfort the mother?
We know not.

Only the hands speak to us.
A gentle touch –
Encouraging,
Reassuring,
Affirming.

A sacred encounter,
An intimate moment
Not to be exposed
To indiscreet eyes.
The only witness,
The strong protecting wood,
Held in their embrace

Silent words.

no words

I t is hard to stand by and see a child, a friend, a loved-one struggle with life.

Sometimes it is difficult even to say the right thing. Often we don't even know what to say. We would like to spare those we love the burden of carrying their own crosses.

Love is utterly vulnerable, completely defenceless, open to whatever comes. To love is to set people free to follow the demands of God, whatever the cost. All we can do is be there, just being… consoling… supporting… showing respect. These are sacred moments.

themes and scripture

The Journey of the Cross | **4th Station** | **Jesus meets his mother**

- No words
  Lk 2:19-20; 34-35; 48-50; (Mt 16:21, 23; Mk 8:31-33)

- Healing touch
  Jn 3:16;15; 12-14; Rm 5:6-8; Ph 2:5-11 Lk 2:34

We pray...

Lord Jesus,
your mother shared
your pain,
your destiny.

As so often we hurt
those we love,
and fail
those we hold dear,
help us to share
in the healing power
of your love.

They seized
a passer-by,
Simon of Cyrene,
who was coming
from the
countryside,
to carry his cross.

Mark 15: 21

unison

Travellers on the same road
Under the one same load.
Body upholding body,
Shoulder to shoulder,
Cheek by cheek:
Twinned as one.

Carrying the same weight
They become one.

Their eyes fixed in the one direction
They strive onward,
Towards the same goal.

There is a need to stay close
To one another.
Synchronising their pace,
Gaining strength –
The beam on their shoulders
Is heavy!
Any shift in weight,
Any disharmony
Will weaken them both.

Together as one!
Is it by love,
Friendship,
Solidarity
Or simply by chance?

Whatever brought them close
Is irrelevant –
Under the same weight
They are as one.

unison

Our streets are crowded with people struggling under the weight they carry. Degradation, desperation, hunger, violence, abuse... Do we have the courage to stop, to get involved? Perhaps we would rather keep our distance. Strangers, refugees? Are they any concern of ours? Who is my neighbour?

What happens around us affects us all in one way or another. Called to be one, our command is to love one another. We owe each other love and support. Simon of Cyrene can inspire us: by accepting to help a stranger, he became as one with Jesus, the Son of God.

themes and scripture

The Journey of the Cross | 5th Station | Simon, a stranger helps Jesus

- Unison
  Lk 23:26; Mt 11:28-30. 27:31; Mk 15:21; Gal 6:2

- Discipleship
  Mt 3:11, 28; Lk 9:57-62; Hb 11:13; Eph 5:1; Ph 3:20-21

We pray...

Lord, as we journey

help us to see

those who stagger

along the path

of the cross:

the refugees,

the homeless,

the lonely.

We ask for

strong shoulders

on which to ease

the load of others

and a heart

filled with love

for all.

I tell you solemnly,
in so far as you
did this
to the least
of my brothers
and sisters,
you did it to me.

Matthew 25: 40

true icon

A gesture of love.
And the spotless linen,
Soaked with blood,
Reveals the features
Of a wounded man.
A Suffering figure,
An enduring face,
At peace.

A woman,
In mourning robe,
Her face screened by
The linen she holds,
Tenderly,
Compassionately,
Displays the shroud
Resting on her chest –
Imprinted as part of her very being.

An empty cracked bowl,
Seemingly emerging
From the body
Whose face is fixed
On the linen,
Held up for all to see.

Whose hands?
We can guess,
By the colour of the skin.

Whose empty cracked bowl?

true icon

Where do we see the face of Christ today? Is it to be found in artistic reproductions? No. He told us where we can see his face. If only we have the courage to look at those who are hungry, those who are naked, those who are lonely, imprisoned; the least, the last... there we see Jesus himself. A gesture of love to release the pain of these brothers and sisters restores in us our likeness to Jesus.

We often hear of heroic acts which helped save the lives of many. How often though do we hear of the simple acts of love, the little ways in which love is shown? Being beside someone on his or her way to death and mopping their brow is a simple yet love filled, intimate act, which can only bring us closer to Christ.

themes and scripture

The Journey of the Cross | 6th **Station** | Veronica, a gesture of love

- True icon
  Mt 25:32-45; Lk 10:16; Jn 13:34-35

- Compassionate love
  Jn 3:16. 15:12-14; Rm 5:6-8; Ph 2:5-11; Lk 2:34

We pray...

Lord, help us

to recognise you

in the hidden corners

of our world.

In the forgotten ones,

those who mean

so little to the world,

whose presence

is never greeted

with a smile.

We ask that we might

reflect your love

for all people in

everything that we do.

*Anyone
who does not
carry his cross
and come after me,
cannot be
my disciple.*

Luke 14: 27

with us

Rough hewn,
Heavy beams
Hammering, forcing the shoulders
Of those who carry them.
So great the strain,
So grotesque
The misshapen bodies beneath.

The throng emerge
As an unseen multitude
Beneath the horizon
Bathed in pale light.

Different races, peoples
Prostrate on their knees.
Heaving their own load –
They have no escape.

Someone surges forward,
Fixing gazing eyes
On the One who leads the way.
In him a difference.
With his arms
Embracing the rough wood
That bends him down.
He seems to have a purpose
He seems to know the sense...
On his knees,
He draws them all.

with us

Pressures from society, our peers, and possibly even our weak wills may stop us from being a true follower of Jesus. It can be difficult to lead the way; yet we know the exhilaration of winning a race, or struggling for what is right in life. We know what we should do and yet we carry on doing the things we shouldn't.

It may be difficult for us today to see any value in the cross. Suffering is a great mystery to us. We may have feelings of helplessness and find ourselves only able to ask *Why*? And yet the choice remains with us. Do we allow ourselves to be crushed beneath the weight of our daily cross, or do we pick ourselves up, and follow in the way of Jesus?

themes and scripture

The Journey of the Cross | 7ᵗʰ **Station** | **Jesus falls with many**

- With us
  Is 41:10-13; Mt 11:28-30; 12:15-21

- The journey of life
  Is 50:9-10. 53:4-7; Mt 3:11,28; Lk 9:57-62; Hb 11:13; Eph 5:1; Ph 3:20-21

We pray...

Lord,

to pick up our cross

and follow you

is a difficult request.

It may be that

in today's world

our responsibilities

are our crosses.

Whatever the cross

may we understand

that only

with you

the burden

is light.

Daughters
of Jerusalem,
do not weep for me,
but weep
for yourselves
and
for your children

Luke 27: 28

nurturing

Mothers weeping,
Lamenting
By the well-worn path
Trodden daily by the convicted
Being led to death.

Injustice manifest
Before their very eyes:
An innocent seized,
An horrendous crime.

They know him –
A firstborn child,
Nurtured by his mother
Like a sapling.
He lived among them
Curing their ills,
Soothing their pain,
Embracing their children.

Should evil be returned for good?

Mothers of the world
Do not weep for me,
Weep for yourselves,
Weep for your children.

Look at your vulnerable offspring,
The children you nurtured in your womb.
Can you spare them from the violence of war?
From devastation of nuclear attacks?
From barbed wire
That tortures their flesh?

Mothers weeping and lamenting
On the roads of the world.
Your cry resounds
Throughout all of history:
It is heard
In Ramah… in Bethlehem…
In Hiroshima… in Auschwitz…
In Kosovo… in Rwanda…
In Darfur… in Afganistan and Iraq…

There is no end to the tears
Running from your eyes.

Mothers on the journey of life,
Trust the green wood,
The innocent Son
Who has strength
To carry your sorrow,
To give your children hope.

nurturing

Mothers, women, they know the pain of loving. In the face of human sorrow and tragedy, mothers are those who pay the highest price of seeing their own children, flesh of their flesh, being deprived of their dignity, abused, tortured, killed. Mothers know the hard way of the cross.

The cross – this horrible means of torture of the past has been replaced with modern and more sophisticated means of mass destruction. Yet Jesus calls women to nurture a better world, so to spare humanity from even greater tragedy.

Indeed, he calls us all to have a mother-like heart, to nurture life around us.

themes and scripture

The Journey of the Cross ▌ 8th Station ▌ Jesus meets the women

- Nurturing
  Lk 23:27-32; Is 66:12-13; Jer 9:16-19; Ho 11:2-4

- Motherhood
  Lk 23:27-32; Jn 3:16. 15:12-14; Rm 5:6-8; Ph 2:5-11; Lk 2:34

We pray...

Jesus,

you are

the beginning

and the end,

the One

who leads us

out of death

into life.

Help us be people

who nurture,

giving life

to those

who feel abandoned

or let down

in any way.

*His yoke
is on my neck,
he has
deprived me
of strength.*

Lamentation 1:14

amen!

The weight of the whole world!
Pressed on the dust of the road
Rejected
Wasted.
The thick timber
Holding his neck –
Pinned like a mouse in its trap!

Who could ever arise again
After such a fall!

No one passing by
No weeping women
No consoling friends
No mother's touch
To comfort, to reassure…
Not even the jeering throng.

Crushed and alone.
Where is God?

Mingled with the dust of the earth
Held down
Exhausted.
Under the vastness
The immensity
Of a dark, blank sky.

Can anyone ever stand again
After such a fall?

The One who trusts.

Far above
Light
Bathing the wood,
Resting on his face.

amen!

In everyone's life there are moments of inner loneliness, a rejection no words can describe. It is the isolation of the aged, the loss of a dear one, the collapse of a family's fortune, the horror of war, the loss of a job, the breaking of a relationship, dreams not coming true... Weighed down by the awfulness of it all, we feel like worms trampled under foot!

Jesus experienced this emptiness as we do... human struggling. But he drank the chalice to the very dregs, still trusting in the Father's unfailing love. With him we will be able to rise up from the struggles that bind us and continue on our way to our final goal.

themes and scripture

The Journey of the Cross | **9th Station** | **Jesus falls again –**
The fall of the world!

- Amen!
  Jb 1:20-21; Lm 3:1-9; Lk 22:39-41

- Trust
  Ps 25, Ps 69; Ps 77; Ps 121

We pray...

Lord Jesus,

when all looks to be

too much,

when we feel

overburdened by life,

when nothing

makes sense any longer,

allow the warmth

of your love

to touch us.

Give us the strength

to say our amen!

to God and to trust

in the Father's care.

They took
Jesus' clothing
and divided it
into four shares.

John 19: 23

whose?

Deprived of its oneness,
Stained with blood,
A seamless white robe,
Pulled from its four corners,
Torn at the centre
Forming a cross.

Three Church leaders finely attired
Claiming ownership of the cloth,
Holding it tightly, even comfortably.
Misled in their belief –
Blind to one another,
Each thinking he owns the lot.

Bloodied,
And fluttering like a flag
The fourth corner.
A black figure,
Marching, striving ahead.
Eager to reach out?

At the foot of the cross
The seamless white robe
Each part weakened,
Divided, spread out –
Yet held together
By the shadow of that same cross.

whose?

Before his passion Jesus prayed that we may be one. Yet division and war among his followers have marked the history of Christianity. Blood has been shed in Jesus' name too often, by too many claiming to possess the true faith, Jesus himself.

Our divisions are the crosses on which Jesus continues to die. Very often our diversity becomes division. Diversity is a gift of the Spirit and enriches the whole body, while division is the work of the evil one and impoverishes us all. 'There is one body, one baptism, one faith'. We belong to one another.

Every day we have the opportunity to work for unity and peace within ourselves, our family, our Churches. Or we may refuse to love our brothers and sisters, deepening the mark of the cross in our world.

themes and scripture

The Journey of the Cross | 10th Station | Jesus is stripped, his garment divided

- Whose?
  Ps 22:18; Mt 27:35; Mk 15:24; Lk 23:34; Jn 19: 23-24
  (Mt 12:25; Mk 3:24-27; Lk 11:17)

- A call to unity
  Jn 17: 20-23; 15: 4-5; Eph 3: 14-21; 1 Cor 3: 4-9

We pray...

Lord, our ways

are not peaceful ways.

Fill us

with your Spirit,

that we may truly

become your people,

the one body

of Christ.

Heal our divisions

and give us courage

to work for unity

and peace.

All who see me
jeer at me,
they sneer
and wag
their heads.

cf Psalm 22

face to face

The sunlight thickens
Colours fade,
The sky darkens.
Why?

What are the people looking at?
Or rather, who is looking at them?
The Man being crucified,
Lying below...

The Roman soldier's arm
Clad with armour,
Brandishing the hammer,
Relentlessly striking on the nail
Penetrating the flesh.

A reaction at each heavy blow:
Compassion
Mockery
Grief
Condolence
Sneering
Dismay
Horror
Scorn.
Each face is different.

Some faces are shielded,
Unable to bear the sight.
Some scrutinise the scriptures
In an attempt to make some sense...
'Wild bulls encircle me
Strong bulls surround me'...
All the while the sun darkens
And the sky grows dimmer.

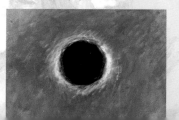

face to face

There are moments in each one's life when we feel as though we are 'nailed', as if on a cross, unable to move, totally at the mercy of others. It may be because of sickness, disability, fear, violence, physical or physiological hurts.

When we feel helpless we come face to face with our own truth and the truth of those around us. We can become victims of others or we may make others pay the price of our indifference, of our insensitivity. As we look at the faces of those around Jesus, as he is being nailed on the cross, can we see ourselves?

themes and scripture

The Journey of the Cross | **11ᵗʰ Station** | **Jesus is nailed to the cross**

- Face to face
  Mt 27:39-44; Mk 15:29-32; Lk 23:35-38; Ps 22:6-13; Ps 27:7-14

- The hour of truth
  Mt 26:14-16. 69-75. 27:20-24; Lk 10:19-37; Jn 8:1-11

We pray...

Lord of love

and compassion,

help us

to be true

to ourselves

and to others.

Give us a

sensitive heart

to ease

the burden

of those who

can't help themselves.

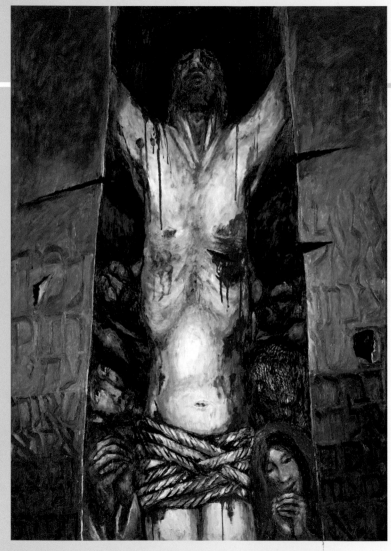

*My God,
my God,
why have you
forsaken me?*

Matthew 27:46

holocaust

Tortured,
Bleeding,
Wracked by pain
And so stretched
That his bones can be counted.
Thick ropes
Securing the body
To its torments.

Head cast toward the darkness;
Mouth releasing
A loud scream against the sky.

The ancient cry,
Eli Eli lama Sabacthani?
Will no longer be read –
It is now heard in the violent scream
That rips apart the sacred scroll.
Tearing the curtain of the temple
From top to bottom.

It is accomplished!
The ancient covenant,
Giving way to the new one.
In his blood.

The crowds appalled
Turning away from him –
So disfigured did he look
Seemingly no longer human...

Without beauty, without majesty,
A thing despised, rejected by people
Struck by God...

Who can bear this sight?
Who has the strength to stand by?
A mother
A friend
A disciple.

holocaust

A s scripture says, 'You didn't accept sacrifices and holocausts… you gave me a body'. Here is the body of Christ, the innocent victim who takes upon himself the human sorrow. Jesus dying on the cross. His whole being stretched to the limits of human bearing. His tortured body recalls the torments of millions of men, women and even little children, in Nazi concentration camps; past and present victims of racism, hatred and war.

Violence is becoming a commonplace experience in our homes. We run the risk of becoming used to the horrible scenes of violence shown by the media: brutalised bodies of children, old people and young, victims of terrorism and wars… We are becoming so accustomed to what we see, that we can watch undisturbed, making no distinction between fiction and reality. Even worse, we may be among those who inflict violence, to a greater or lesser degree, or we could be onlookers doing nothing to stop the violence.

themes and scripture

The Journey of the Cross | 12th Station | **Jesus dies on the cross**

- Holocaust
  Hb 10:5-7; Ps 22:1; Ps 40:6-8; Mt 27:45-56; Mk 15:33-41; Lk 23:44-49; 6-8

- The folly of God
  Jn 3:15-16; Rm 5:6-11; 8:31-34; 1 Cor 2:23-26; Eph 1:3-8; 2: 1-6; Hb 12:18-29

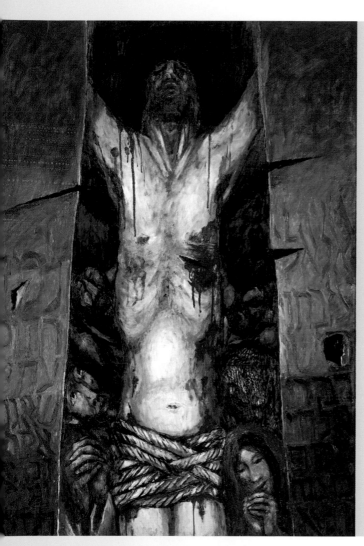

We pray...

Lord,

dying you destroyed

our death,

rising you restored

our life.

Fill our hearts

with your courage

so that we no longer

remain bystanders

but can be counted

among those

who work

for justice

and peace.

Peace be with you,
my own peace
I give you;
a peace
which the world
cannot give,
this is my gift
to you.

John 14:27

maternal womb

All is fulfilled!
Now there are
No cries of sorrow
No pain, no struggle.
A corpse finally at peace,
Secure in his mother's embrace.

Silence
Intimacy
Peace.

A mother, tenderly
Enfolding the child of her womb,
Cherishing his blood-stained body;
Naked as the day
She gave him birth.

Now she hushes him
Into the dawn of a new birth.

The skulls of our forebearers,
A symbol of death,
Now superseded
By the new creation.

A new dawn
Filtering through new life.

The dove,
Bearing an olive branch,
Announces
The new covenant of peace.
His gift to all.

maternal womb

O f all women you are the most blessed, and blessed is the fruit of your womb. These words must have resounded in Mary's heart so many times as the mystery of Jesus unfolded day by day. How can we call *blessed* a mother whose child has been persecuted, maltreated and who ends up dead on a cross?

Mary is blessed because she believed in the faithfulness of God. Truly she personifies the maternal womb of God, that nurturing love, which gave Jesus' life over death and charges us with newness of life. The life of the children of God.

Can we trust God? Can we feel loved and blessed, held together in his continuous bond of love? Even when touched by suffering and death?

themes and scripture

The Journey of the Cross | 13th Station | Jesus in his mother's arms

- Maternal womb
  Jn 19:25-27. 32-35. Jn 3:3-4; 15-16; Lk 1:42. 11:28

- He is our peace
  Rm 5:10-11; Cl 1:15-20; Eph 1:3-7; 2:14-18

We pray...

Lord of life,

we pray with Mary,

give us faith

to love

when our hearts

feel cold.

Give us hope

when all seems lost,

and trust

when we feel bereft.

In Jesus, may we find

the source

of our new life

and our peace.

*Unless the grain
of wheat
falls into the earth
and dies
it remains
a single grain.
If it dies
it yields
a rich harvest.*

John 12:24

chrysalis

The burial cloth
Translucent
Revealing
A body at rest.
The face at peace.
Wounded hands
Marked with red blood.

Inside, the tomb is dark and spacious.
Outside, the promise of a bright warm
morning.

The light is breaking
Through the stone
Which seals the entrance.
Within the linen cloths
The body dazzles,
Like –
    A pearl in the oyster shell
    A chrysalis in its cocoon
    A seed in germination
    An embryo in the womb.
The inexplicable
Untouchable
Invisible
Recreating energy!
Into the soil,
Swollen with new life.

chrysalis

S o often we feel the failures of our hopes, our dreams, our plans. Our efforts may appear empty and our attempts fruitless. The stone is rolled across the entrance to our hearts, on our relationships, our whole life – the stone shuts everything out.

Yet, unless the grain of wheat dies, it bears no fruit. Baptised in Christ, rooted in him, we are bearers of his new life. We carry God's reassurance that with him nothing is impossible.

themes and scripture

The Journey of the Cross | 14th Station | Jesus lies buried

- Chrysalis (like a...)
  Mt 27:57-60; Jn 19:38-42; Mk 15:42-46; Lk 23:52-55

- Charged with life
  Mt 13:31-32. 44; Jn 11:25-26. 12:24; Rm 6:4-5; Eph 1:20; Cl 2:12-13

We pray...

Help us to believe,
Lord,
that ends are
but beginnings
and that graves are
but the doorways
to a new life.

For you are
the Lord
of the living
and the dead.

Woman,
why are you
weeping?
Who
are you
looking for?....

John 20:11-18

alive!

A familiar scene:
Signs of death all around,
A woman kneeling,
Mourning
By the tomb of the beloved.

Jesus, the Nazarene.
A name carved in the stone:
His death, a violent one
His tomb among
The million graves
Dotted all over,
In the farthest flung places
Of our world.

Mary of Magdala.
You must have come a long way.
Your bare feet
Tell the story of your journeying
Through the night,
To touch the stone
Of the One you loved,
And who is no more.

Woman,
Why do you seek him
Among the dead?
Why are you weeping?
Look at the sky.

Can't you see?
The light of a new bright dawn
Dispells the darkness
Of the night.
Breaking down walls.

Death is defeated.
Graves bathed in light.
Warmed, awakened.

That light shines on you,
Almost too much to bear.
Can't you hear?
He is calling you by name.

Mary,
Woman,
Go and tell my brothers,
Tell everyone:
I am alive!

alive!

Jesus lived among us, suffered, died and was buried like one of us. His tomb, one of our tombs. His name among others names. Yet, 'Why do you look among the dead?'... Because we feel more comfortable with these *facts*, they are within our reach – nobody can dispute that we do die. When the stone is put in place, it seems as though it is a dead end.

Jesus reaches out in our despair and calls us to see – he is risen! His is an empty tomb, as ours are empty tombs. We are destined to live. The light of his resurrected body, charges with new life our vision of death. Death has no longer power over him, nor has it over us. He calls us, as he called Mary, to go and spread this wonderful news.

themes and scripture

A Path to Light

- Alive!
  Jn 20:11-18; Mt 28:9-10; Mk 16:9-11; Phil 2:5-11; 1 Cor 3:22

- We are Easter people
  Jn 11:25-26; Rm 8:17-18; Eph 2:1-10; 4:17-5:20; Cl 1:12-20; 3:1-4

We pray...

Risen Lord,

fill our hearts

with your Easter joy.

May the light

of your new life

shine forth from us,

so that we may

fill the world

with the good news

of your resurrection.

Dying you destroyed

our death,

rising you

restored our life.

'Come
and have breakfast.
Then Jesus
said to Simon,
'Do you love me...?'

cf John 21: 12,15

plenitude

Enfolded by the light
Of a sky splendid, shining.
Lit by a charcoal fire.

In the distance
Tiny boats
Heavy with an abundant
Miraculous catch.

There is plenty!
Come and help.
Come and see.
Come and eat.

What do you see, Peter,
As you emerge from the water?
Is someone calling you?
There on the shore.

Warming by the fire,
You denied him before,
You said you didn't know
Who he was!

Yet in the light of this charcoal
By the brightness dawning on this new day
You know him now –
It is the Lord!
He is calling you again,
Do not hesitate.
Leave behind the darkness of your shame,
This is the light of a new dawn.

The fire is burning
The bread is broken again.
There is plenty.
Come!

plenitude

Our lives are charged with the light of the Risen Lord. We are wrapped in light, we are children of the light. Yet at times we live our lives in the shadow of our empty efforts, of our failures, of our lack of faith. Especially when we can't forgive ourselves for failing God himself. We can't see the light around us!

It is there, in the midst of our daily routines that the power of the resurrection works in us. The Risen Lord reaches out to us as he did with the disciples on the seashore. He reassures us that our sins are forgiven, our failures are no more – he has paid the price and we are redeemed, we are a new creation. He urges us to love and to trust: 'Do you love me?'. 'Forget about the past: come, warm yourselves, eat with me'.

themes and scripture

A Path to Light

- Plenitude
  Jn 21:1-17; Lk 5:4-11. 24:36-43

- The Bread of life
  Is 25:6-12. 55:1-3; Mt 7:7-11. 26:26-29

We pray...

Risen Lord,

the power

of your new life

overwhelms us.

May we greet

with joy the news that

we are reconciled.

You who call us friends,

warm our pounding

hearts with the fire

of your love and feed us

with the food

that really satisfies.

They said
to each other,
'Did not
our hearts burn
within us
as he talked to us
on the road
and explained
the scriptures
to us'?

Luke 24:32

understanding

The bread is blessed and broken,
And eyes open!

His body bathed in dazzling light
Hidden from your sight.
His presence fills
The room,
Warms the heart.
Now the Word comes clear.
You understand.

How can you tell the story
To the brothers and sisters
You left in Jerusalem?
How can you describe him?

A pilgrim on your way,
When fearful and disillusioned
You made a move back
To the dreary life
You had left behind
To follow the One
Who was to be
The fulfilment of all dreams?

An illusion,
A bluff.
He was arrested,
Tortured,
Dead on a cross.
Defeat!

A pilgrim on your way,
He discloses
The sense of it all:

You foolish men!
Was it not ordained that
The Christ should suffer
To enter his glory?

Hearts on fire,
New hope enkindles.
Stay with us!

At table once again,
He breaks the bread:
Take it, eat it.

Now you can see!
But he has gone.

How
Can you describe Him?

Light!
God who is light
And in his light
We shall see the Light.

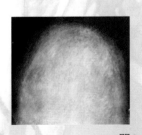

understanding

A s we journey into life, we carry the memory of the events that touch us most. We walk the road of Emmaus – disappointed, we want to make a radical move away from our past. Our friends mean nothing to us any more, we have nothing in common that can hold us together. We feel let down even by God. Who is this Jesus we believe in, if being a follower of him is to find ourselves in trouble, to be losers against the power of this world? Our hope is dead!

We are blessed if, though heavy in our heart, we carry the memory of what hurts. If we can talk about it, if we can be true, we are blessed. If we still carry the longing that moves us on, we are blessed. The risen Jesus walks with us, he listens to us, stays with us. He breaks open the Word of God, and breaks the bread that gladdens our hearts. At table with him, we understand the meaning of our life, the sense of his mystery.

themes and scripture

The Path of Light

- Understanding
  Lk 24:13-35; Jn 2:1-5; Acts 5:27-32.40-41 1 Pt 1:17-21

- The eucharist
  Jn 6:35, 41, 48, 50, 57-58; 1Cor 10:14.11:24-26; Acts: 2:42-46

We pray...

Jesus, our companion,

our friend, our God.

Thank you for journeying

with us, staying with us.

Open the eyes of our mind

that we may understand

the mystery of your dying

and living.

Fill us with joy

when we sit at the table

of your Eucharist

where you sustain us

with your Word and

nourish us with the

bread of life.